GIPPI[NG]
JOURNEYS

A Personal Anthology

JOHN PLAYER

i

CONTENTS

Employment in retirement,
I drive, walk, eat and write,
Keeping mind and body active,
I'll not give up the fight.

BY THE SAME AUTHOR

The Amorphous School

Paper in Defining the Curriculum: Histories and Ethnologies,
Ivor Goodson and Stephen Ball (1984)

Under the pseudonym of JACK WEBB

Cedric's Busy Week

The Adventures of Cedric the Spider (2018)

Cedric's Holiday

The Further Adventures of Cedric the Spider (2019)

Cedric's Christmas

The Festive Adventures of Cedric the Spider (2020)

Doctor Goblins

The Power of Cobalus (2021)

ACKNOWLEDGEMENTS

My grateful thanks go to Mark Braithwaite, managing Director of Gipping Occupational Health for permitting me to use references to the company and photographs of the Mobile Health Unit.

DEDICATION

This book is dedicated to my wife, Brenda, to our dear family and many friends, and to all those work colleagues, past and present, whose names appear in this anthology.

INTRODUCTION

I began to write and self-publish children's books in 2018 at the tender age of seventy-two. Over the next three years and under the pseudonym of Jack Webb, I published a trilogy with the subtitle of 'The Adventures of Cedric the Spider'.

Cedric's Busy Week, Cedric's Holiday and Cedric's Christmas were prompted by a request from my daughter, Emily, to retell the tales I dreamt up as twenty-minute bedtime stories when she was small. Cedric, along with his anthropomorphic toothbrush friends, Belinda and Bertie, was my attempt to encourage Emily and her brother, Edmund, both to clean their teeth and not to be afraid of spiders. The excellent illustrations within these pages were provided by my good friend, neighbour and erstwhile colleague, Gary Stocker.

Gary and I then began work on a more ambitious project based on two mystical woodland characters, the Doctor Goblins Locum and Ten Ends, creatures from folklore which had previously been encountered by Cedric, Belinda and Bertie during their nocturnal forays.

'Doctor Goblins, the Power of Cobalus' was published in 2021 as a single novel rather than a collection of short stories. It also marked the first occasion when all the illustrations were in colour and was intended for an older, more sophisticated age range of children, as well as a fun read for adults.

For the next two years I laboured to write a sequel to Doctor Goblins. After completing ten chapters, 'Doctor Goblins 2', its working title, appeared to be going nowhere. It seemed to lack the inspiration, magic and surrealism which I felt was present in its predecessor.

I found time to write during my part-time, retirement employment as a driver for Gipping Occupational Health, a company based in Needham Market, Suffolk, which provides Occupational Health and Wellbeing services throughout the Eastern Counties. On an occasional basis, I would drive the van, or the unit, the name by which it was most commonly known, to a variety of industrial locations, including factories, joineries, office blocks, building sites, and even sewage farms. At the site I would stabilize, plug in and prepare the unit's rear carriage studio in readiness for the arrival of a nurse, officially entitled an 'Occupational Health Advisor,' who would spend the day performing health checks on the staff. Once testing had commenced, I would be free to leave the site, inevitably on foot, and often involving a journey of several miles, to find a venue for breakfast, usually in a town centre location.

With a full English inside me and a refillable coffee for refreshment, I would take out my Chromebook and spend the morning writing, eventually returning to the unit in mid-afternoon, ready to pack away and drive back to the office.

It was during one of these journeys that my brief career as an author (how pretentious!) took a different turn. It was a cold, damp, drizzly day in February 2023. I had set up the unit at the site of the Aspall Cider House, rustically located in central Suffolk, and was walking along the B1077 towards the bustling village of Debenham, a road which at this point tracks the course of the river Deben. Whilst I anticipated with pleasure the excellent breakfast waiting for me at the charming River Green Café and Deli at the top of the village, I was most certainly not looking forward to battling along drudgingly to complete Chapter 11 of Doctor Goblins 2.

I stopped and gazed down at the river, in full flood after a prolonged period of heavy rain. Just then four words came to mind – 'Fast flows the Deben'.

I had always written poetry, and, at a very young age, my Auntie Jean had introduced me to the 'Cautionary Tales' of Hilaire Belloc. I tried my hand at writing such tales throughout my student days, along with love poems and comic verse. In later life, my working years would give me many an occasion to pen celebratory odes for milestone birthdays and retirements for friends and colleagues, and even satirical pieces lampooning those who deserved such treatment.

At that moment I decided to abandon Doctor Goblins 2, certainly for the moment, perhaps forever. Instead, I would write a sonnet for each of my journeys partaken on behalf of Gipping Occupational Health. Gipping Journeys is the collection of these sonnets, augmented by poetry from my earlier years to complete this anthology.

Fast flows the Deben ... rising near the village of Debenham, Suffolk:

GIPPING JOURNEYS

A collection of sonnets inspired by walks undertaken during my employment with Gipping Occupational Health.

For Brenda

*From Aspall Cider, in the hamlet of Aspall in mid-Suffolk,
to the River Green Café, Debenham village
February 2023*

Fast flows the Deben, swelled by winter flood,
Grey, dreary nimbus obscuring morning sun,
Chilled winds of March perturb the warmest blood,
Drenched paths and fields ere the day's begun.
Walking to the village from Aspall's Cider House,
Following the river, past the broken bridge,
Catching sight of pictures which sombre spirits rouse,
Patches of yellow on the grassy ridge.
Spring around the corner, daffodils in flower,
Primroses smiling, the village now is seen,
The sun breaks through the ever-dwindling shower,
I reach my haven, breakfast, River Green.
What greater pleasure is there, my joy to enhance?
To have my loved one with me, sweet happenstance.

Spirit Yachts

From Spirit Yachts, Ipswich Haven Marina,
to the Cricketers, Crown Street, Ipswich.
March 2023

The scent of wood, marking a yacht's construction,
Sleek, graceful vessels built in Ipswich Port,
Whence I depart this workshop of production,
Through old town treading, bygone days in thought.
Holy thoroughfares, Saints Nicholas and Peter,
Statues nearby Silent Street, eponymous mystery name,
Cardinal Wolsey, both Chancellor and Teacher,
Russian Prince Oblensky, of English rugby fame.
Grandma and the family, in bronze from Giles' cartoons,
Georgian Corn Exchange, where Market Cross once stood.
Across the busy High Street, minstrel busking tunes,
Then once more the Marina, a sailor's livelihood.
Thirty-footer launched today, secured is the mast.
Both town and skilled artisans resurrect the past.

A Living Hotchpotch

*From Sackers (Waste Management), Great Blakenham, a walk which crosses the rail
line to London, bridges the River Gipping and passes beneath the main A14 highway,
ending at the Crown Inn, Claydon.*
April 2023

Blakenham and Claydon, villages the river divides.
Footpath, road and rail line, the valley's routeways tracking,
A living hotchpotch, with house, factory, meadow, side by side,
All life is there, unplanned, harmony and order lacking.
Therein its worldly charm; no veneer, no false glossing.
The grimy scrap metal yard, where this day's walk commences,
Though instantly impeded by the gates of railway crossing
Giving way to moist green fields where nature stirs my senses.
I'm touched by birdsong, horses grazing, river rushing,
With industry intruding, truck, train, tractor blaring,
Lovers holding hands, a kiss, a maiden blushing,
Workmen road repairing, sweating hard and swearing.
Journey's end, the High Street, the Crown Inn, breakfast dining.
Things are as they are, contentment, Spring sun shining.

Raceday in Newmarket

*From Anglia Fabrications and Design Limited, Depot Road, to The Golden
Lion Inn (Wetherspoons), High Street, Newmarket.
April 2023*

Through the lanes and fields of Suffolk, in Spring the hares are
bounding,
I drive to main roads traffic jammed, then reach my destination -
Newmarket, a town renowned for the hooves of horses pounding,
Where stands a factory, workers skilled in metal fabrication.
Through roads named after legends of the turf, my footpath weaves,
Piggott, Gordon Richards, then along the watercourse,
Styled Yellow Brick Road by locals, stud fields my eye perceives,
With stable lads and lasses exercising pure-bred horse.
It's race day here in centre town, first meeting of the year,
Pubs early packed with punters contemplating food and form,
While factory makes a staircase, balustrade and iron pier,
The stable nurtures thoroughbreds to take the race by storm.
They're off! - from town to racecourse shortly after lunch.
They can't all back a winner, but each can have a hunch!

Oundle

*From the sports pavilion at Oundle School to the centre of town, with an
overnight stay at the Talbot Hotel, where, it is rumoured, Mary Queen of Scots
still today descends the staircase supposedly removed from Fotheringhay Castle.
May 2023*

As I gaze through the window, sat at my breakfast table
In the Greedy Piglet, cafe in Oundle town,
There passes a flurry of scholars, both studious and able,
The girls in baggy culottes, flowing to ankles down.
The boys in blazers blue, their neckties smartly tethered,
With folders in their arms, they represent the pride,
These youthful peacocks, elegantly feathered,
Of the English Public School, with no resource denied.
Contemporary leisure structures where my gentle stroll begins,
Acres of sporting grassland and pool where athletes train,
To historic centre town, limestone buildings fit for kings,
The Tudor Hotel Talbot tied with Scots Queen Mary's reign.
I'm resting there tonight, with its ancient oaken stair
From Fotheringhay Castle, but will I see her there?

JOHN PLAYER

East Suffolk

From PPC Broadband Fibres Ltd., Parham Airfield to
Marlesford Farm Shop and Café.
June 2023

May becomes June, yet the chilled east winds still blow,
As I walk from the airfield where wartime planes once flew.
A flat expanse of farmland where shoots of spring wheat grow,
Small lanes bordered by hedgerows, with dog rose peeping through.
This is the colour time, green trees still dressed in bloom,
The pink and cream horse chestnuts, the hawthorn coated white,
The pretty cottage garden, the lilac's purple plume,
The golden chain laburnum restoring spring sunlight.
I pass through Marlesford village, with pantile rooves abundant,
Anticipating breakfast, to Farm Shop Café called,
Crossing major road with train station now redundant,
With bridge for trickling stream, the Ore flows to the Alde.
With weary limbs I sit to eat, my travels but half ended,
The Farm Shop Suffolk breakfast? Highly recommended!

Servants In Contrast

*From Ellingham Grain Store near Bungay, Suffolk, by lanes and footpaths to
Kirby Cane Post Office, shortly after the Administration Team Leader,
Amanda Heavens, left Gipping Occupational Health.
June 2023*

Down tree-lined rural lanes I gently wend my way
From mighty, iron grain store, which incongruously grew
Midst such lush verdant meadows, in which my musings stray
To one who lately left us, herself for pastures new.
I see her as I traipse along through rape seed pods and weeds,
Amanda, appositely gifted with the surname Heavens,
With graceful calm and kindliness, she met our office needs.
While I and those around her were all at six' and sevens.
I pass St Mary's Church, a full six centuries built,
The village football ground, the local Primary school,
The Waveney flowing by, rich soil of sand and silt,
Grain crops in abundance, Suffolk's harvest fuel.
Sweet lady from our office to you we bid farewell,
And the ugly metal grain store? Both have served us well.

The Inspiration of Bury St. Edmunds

From Quality Castings, a foundry in Bury St. Edmunds,
to the town centre and Corn Exchange (Wetherspoons).
July 2023

Verdant summer foliage adorns this handsome town,
With hollyhocks and honeysuckle my footpath richly bordered.
Avenues with linden, maple, and horse chestnut crown,
Houses, shops and factories most neatly groomed and ordered.
In Fordham Road, mediaeval ruin, an early Gothic door,
Once the Hospital of St Saviour, with wall base excavated,
Founded by Abbot Sampson to shelter priest and poor.
Was Humphrey, Duke of Gloucester, murdered here? It stands
debated.
From Conquest days so much remains, the ancient Moyse's Hall,
A museum now, but years gone by, both workhouse and a jail.
In the beauteous Abbey Gardens, Norman ruins still stand tall.
As does the tower at Abbey Gate, unchanged in time and scale.
From barren path and crevice, somehow, hollyhocks spring high,
Just as this town inspires my empty thoughts and verse to fly.

Poundfield

Poundfield Precast Ltd sits adjacent to Grove Farm, Creeting St Peter, a village on the outskirts of Stowmarket. Nearby lies the vast construction site for Gateway 14, soon to become the largest business, innovation and logistics park in East Anglia. Gipping Occupational Health Advisors regularly perform health checks for Poundfield's staff.
July 2023

A precast concrete factory with everything displayed,
Heavy trucks and forklifts, great heaps of sand and shingle,
Wood piles, rods of metal, men wielding shovel and spade,
Where Hi Viz jackets, helmets, even smart suits intermingle.
In contrast lie the fields around, with wheat and barley sown,
As rural Suffolk loses ground along the Gipping vale,
Vast building sites emerge in which huge warehouses have grown,
With truckloads of materials conveyed by road and rail.
Giant moulded precast blocks engulf the Poundfield site,
As does cement dust coating each roadway, roof and lorry,
Our Gipping nurse tests workers for hearing, lungs and sight,
Making sure that all work safely; better safe than sorry.
Industrial growth on such a scale generates work and wealth,
But let it not be harmful to environment and health.

Knotty Ash

*My Senior Citizen's Bus Pass took me on a journey of some ten miles from
Knotty Ash Woodworking Ltd at Manor Farm, Great Chesterford, to
Cambridge City centre for breakfast at The Regal, a Wetherspoon's Pub.
September 2023*

A joinery on Manor Farm, where craftsmen ply their trade
For television studio and hotel front reception,
With saw and drill machinery, the finest desks are made,
Bespoke for every customer and finished to perfection.
Too far to walk, I catch a bus, an hour to Cambridge city,
With ancient university, its pride, King's College Chapel,
Down narrow lanes, with Tudor beams, straw thatch a picture pretty,
Early browned horse chestnut leaves and ripening pear and apple.
Through wealthy rural villages with English cottage garden,
Ickleford, then Duxford, museum of war imperial,
The morning mist now lifting as Autumn starts to harden,
The fields of gold - just straw bales now, harvest cropped the cereal.
From workshop in a rural barn to illustrious Magdalen College
I trace the skills of the artisan to the academic's knowledge.

10

Passionate About Packaging

*Two nights at The Poplars Hotel, in the village of Moulton, Northamptonshire,
driving the GOH unit to FFP Packaging Ltd on Moulton Park Industrial
Estate, followed by a No. 7 bus ride into Northampton town centre.
September 2023*

Ironstone cottages line the streets with garden walls to match,
As I wend my way through Moulton, down narrow twisting lanes.
The rustic, sandy buildings, some capped with rooves of thatch,
A mediaeval parish church where Norman nave remains.
An early drive to FFP which proudly boasts the banner
People, Passion, Packaging with tailor-made solution
For every type of product wrap, whatever shape or manner,
A state of art production line, reliable distribution.
I take the bus to Northampton town and through its window gaze,
The bustling world outside reflects a mayhem of variety,
School, factory, church and restaurant, new building sites, a maze
Of people young and old, a multicultural society.
Yet the cynic deep inside suggests that people with a passion
For packaging and bubble wrap are treated with compassion!

The Drabbet Smock

*From the Suffolk and Essex Joinery, Haverhill, for breakfast at The Drabbet
Smock, one of my favourite Wetherspoon establishments, where Gary Stocker,
my book illustrator, and I were photographed for an article in Wetherspoon
News in the Spring 2022 edition. Drabbet Smock? All will be revealed!
October 2023*

The Suffolk and Essex Joinery creates for the interior,
Fitting out for retail, commercial and the arts,
Designed and built with ancient skills by artisans superior,
I watch with wonder, breathe the scent which new sawn wood
imparts.
As post-war London claimed more fields and grew in population,
Within reach of the capital, towns grew to house the overspill.
Estates sprang up for those misplaced, with sorry reputation,
So often wrongly justified, such is the case with Haverhill.
From joinery to Drabbet Smock, my customary habit,
The name reflects its rustic past when farmers' smocks were twined,
From unbleached yellow fabric, coarse linen known as drabbet,
A wholesome breakfast venue, no better could I find.
Employment in retirement, I drive, walk, eat and write,
Keeping mind and body active, I'll not give up the fight.

12

A Bad Start

Gipping Occupational Health's customer, Durman Stearn, a civil engineering company based in Cottenham near Cambridge, requested that health checks in the unit could be best conducted at Cambridge Rugby Club, a more spacious location. Durman Stearn has improved the driveway infrastructure at the club and remains a sponsor. Unfortunately, stand-still traffic on the approach roads and a postcode which caused my sat-nav to misdirect me down an adjacent street leading to narrow gravel tracks, resulted in a late arrival on site. Moreover, the parking space allotted for the unit had no electricity causing a further delay while we were relocated. Despite these problems, health tests were delayed by just five minutes.
October 2023

Satellites in the exosphere signal our navigation,
Sat-Nav replacing folded maps on journeys made by road.
This day the Cambridge Rugby Club the chosen destination,
But shared by tracks to nowhere within the same postcode!
A shaky start but soon forgot, the walk to city clear.
In Newnham Road, Domenico's, Gentleman's Hairdresser**,
Cross Sheep's Green to the River Cam, punts resting by the weir,
St Benet's Church with Saxon roots from Edward the Confessor,
Today, however, oft ignored, as tourists make their way
Towards King's College Chapel, its architecture lyrical,
With stained glass and fan vaulting to take the breath away,
In Silver Street, across the Cam, Newton's Bridge Mathematical.
The rugby fields, the landmarks, grand college in every street,
Provides work for lowly labourer employed by the elite.

** Why this line? I liked the shop front!

Shopfront Symmetry

Mathematical Bridge, Cambridge

14

Lakenheath Fen

To Murfitts Industries' factory adjacent to Lakenheath Station and RSPB
Lakenheath Fen. Murfitts claim to recycle 100% of 20 million tyres every year.
October 2023

This day I drive to Suffolk west, where forest turns to fen,
Through Elveden to Lakenheath, bleak autumn, flat and damp,
Yet sanctuary for wildlife, inspiration for my pen,
The beauty of the Little Ouse, wetlands, the marsh fowl camp.
Adjacent to the bird reserve a mighty factory stands,
Where road tyres are recycled, a myriad of uses,
Surfaces for playparks, rubber granules, steel bands,
Incongruously set amidst the ditches and the sluices.
Just yards away the Breckland line traverses busy main road,
The station here but scarcely used, some two miles from the town,
As is the U.S. air force base, fighters with deadly payload,
The trucks, trains, birds and Lighting jets all flying up and down.
Every hour of every day the factory wheels are grinding,
Just as in daylight skies or night, the fenland birds are winding.

15

Autumn Glory

From Mendlesham, a rural drive on a beautiful autumnal day to HSP Garden Buildings' factory in Mildenhall. My journey took me past the Anglo-Saxon Village in West Stow at the heart of the Brecklands. In the town itself, I visited the parish church of St. Mary's, the largest in Suffolk, a magnificent example of Gothic architecture from the Decorated period with carved wooden angels suspended from its tie beam roof.
November 2023

I drive along enchanted lanes lit up by autumn sun
Through yellow, brown and golden arch of trees at time of fall.
Leaves flutter down around me, the day has scarce begun,
Passing fields and King's Forest en route to Mildenhall.
Once, man would turn to nature to meet his every need,
And West Stow Saxon Village re-enacts those ancient ways,
Forest deer for meat and bone, with honey used for mead,
Wood and straw to build a hut and pen where livestock graze.
Just as plying wood today, the workshop where I'm placed,
A range of garden buildings from summerhouse to shed,
Where craftsmen still wield tools back to their forbears traced.
In town, the grand St. Mary's Church with angels overhead.
Yet Mildenhall's main claim to fame - its giant air force Station,
Though Rocca's Café Lounge will be my breakfast destination!

Container Ships and Fish 'n' Chips

To Indo European Foods, Felixstowe, Britain's largest container port, but also a
traditional English seaside resort. A pleasant walk from the factory took me to
the sea front and the delightfully named Gulliver's Wife's Café for breakfast.
November 2023

Wide, winding Suffolk estuaries into the North Sea flow,
The Deben east, the Orwell north and to the west, the Stour.
Converging at the giant coastal port of Felixstowe
Where sandy seaside town competes with mighty gantry power.
Indo European Foods today my destination,
"A passport to a world of Food" in which "True Taste Unites",
Bold taglines these, with products brought from many a distant
nation
To Anglia's shore, containers hoisted down from lofty heights.
Yet east of Landguard Fort and Point a different town emerges,
Pavilion, pier and pleasure beach, with slot machines and rides,
A glorious day today, the sea is calm, no winter surges,
To Gullivers for breakfast fare, with eager, hungry strides.
Fortune indeed, to venture here, autumn, late November,
No summer crowds, a glowing sky, a fine day to remember.

RITES OF PASSAGE

BIRTH

Lewis James Keeble

The first child of a good friend and colleague, Lewis James Keeble was born three months prematurely weighing just two pounds. Derek, his father, asked me to write a verse thanking the hospital staff who had worked tirelessly to save his life. Louis' partner Coral now works in the same Baby Special Care unit in Colchester Hospital, where the senior nurses still remember Louis' birth.

Mid-March, and spring returns to wood and dale,
Time of renewal; fresh budding from the earth.
Creatures new, some robust, some frail
Just as this child's uncertain, fearful birth.

Into the world, so long before his time,
Came Lewis James, so perfect and so small,
Clinging to life, weak the heartbeat's rhyme,
Shallow the breath, soft the infant call.

2000

19

JOHN PLAYER

Skin translucent, waiting for the flesh
To fill the tiny form, and half-closed eyes,
Still devoid of fluffing brow or lash,
As taken from his mother's arms, he sighs.

Passing to the care of those who heal:
Kindly nurse whose skilled and practised art
To nurture, tend, suffer with and feel
All the pain within a mother's heart.

And consummate physician's gentle touch,
Treating, soothing, remedy and balm,
Restoring health and hope; from little, much,
From weakness, strength; from restless fever, calm.

The weeks go by and summer's golden sun
Begins to traverse heaven's vaulted dome.
Derek and Lisa's darling little one
Is strong enough at last to leave for home.

2023

IN LOVE

1. New dawn, with yesterday's storm subsiding,
A warm and misty peace surrounds my soul.
June morn, air moist and heavy with our love,
My shattered heart now once again made whole.
Bleak winter past, and spring gives way
To eternal burning summer, for us made,
Where waiting for our bodies full entwined,
Lies love's deepest, greenest, most enchanting glade.

So now I see you, through you, clear
Beyond the sweetening sadness of your eyes,
To timeless serenity and lasting grace
Wherein your inner beauty truly lies.
Eternal pool of loveliness,
Nestled in our comely, leafy, radiant bower,
To soothe and quench my aching, raging thirst
And succour new love's softly sprouting flower.

2. I keep thinking of you,
Pouring you into my bowl.
Utterly full of you,
Making me part into whole.

I feel lost without you,
Lonely heart, gaping hole,
Then you pass by my window
And fill my empty soul.

3. The glances over cocktails
That used to be so sweet,
No longer seem so amorous
Across the Shredded Wheat!

21

MARRIAGE

Emily and Jay

*My 'Father of the Bride' speech on the occasion of my daughter Emily's wedding
to James Mclelland-Taylor, August 2016*

Ladies, gentlemen, from far and wide,
I'm John, proud father of the bride.
So many of you! Well, I'm blowed!
I should have gone to Portman Road!
My poetry's bad, my prose is worse,
I'll therefore make this speech in verse
And also on behalf of others,
Louise and Di, our worthy mothers,
Jay's father Ross, now full of pride,
And Brenda, always at my side.

Dear family, friends, guests one and all,
Pray welcome to this nuptial hall.
'A hall?' you say. 'He's being sarcy.
He couldn't find a rhyme for marquee!'
So, in this decorous wedding ROOM,
First greet the family of the groom:
Jay's splendid parents, Ross and Di,
With sons to catch a young girl's eye!
Jay's brother Toby we shall toast,
Our dazzling ceremonial host!
Fresh from Texas, the Lone Star State,
And cousin Heather from Kuwait,
Then Jay himself … to our delight
To Emily his troth did plight.
What's more, he's thirty this very day.
So, let's ALL sing without delay …
(Happy birthday to you …)

To the pride of the McLelland clan,
How pleased we are he's Emily's man!

We welcome, too, on t'other side,
The copious family of the bride.
It won't have escaped your attention,
There are far too many to mention!
But for those who like alliterations
It's odd that most of these relations,
As well as Suffolk can be met
In Sussex, Surrey and Somerset!
Then some from Gloucester's hills and vales
And also Cardiff – that's in Wales!

Though it's near impossible to describe
The complexities of Emily's tribe.
As well as all the normal kin,
The sisters, cousins, aunts and mothers,
Uncles, dads, grandparents, brothers,
Some have a prefix fitted in
Like ex- and step- and even half-,

To map them out you'll need a graph!
Like W.S. Gilbert's sisters and cousins,
They all can be reckoned up by dozens.

But one, our Cathe, we shall applaud.
As anchor girl she struck a chord
With Toby, showing poise and class.
So, let's again all raise a glass …

Greetings then to our relations,
From many and diverse locations!

I'd certainly have to make amends
If I'd left out the many friends
Of Em the bride and bridegroom Jay
Many who've come from far away.
The list of course cannot be thorough,
There's sure to be a passing glitch,
But I must mention Attleborough,
At school where Jay met best man Rich.
Greetings, Rich, it's your turn soon,
Your chance the bridegroom to lampoon.

A kindly welcome to you all,
For those born north of Hadrian's Wall,
And far across the Irish Sea,
Student friends of Emily.
Those of you who've made the hike
From regions west of Offa's Dyke,
And I am told, by word of mouth,
Others from England's north and south.
The brave folk in abundant order,
Who crossed the Suffolk/Norfolk border,
Waving passports, with little pity
For those supporting Norwich City.
Friends from school and work and home,
Where'er my daughter chanced to roam!
Lastly, who from Canada flew,
Emily's Med. School friend, Ken Woo!

So now to exercise my duty
To give away this ravishing beauty!
Funny concept, 'Give Away',
I should have put her on eBay.
The cost of having kids today,
A quick return on my outlay!
I would, of course, have split the sum,
And given half to Emily's mum!
It wasn't - I didn't have the nerve,
I could have set a low reserve,
But postage was prohibitive,
The feedback probably negative.
Then in every sales submission,
You have to comment on condition.
And the only choice was 'used' or 'new'.
The description also must be true.
So 'Daughter, British, twenty-nine,
Suffolk born, superb bloodline,

25

Clever, caring, full of life,
What's more – a doctor for your wife!
At home in the kitchen, loves to bake,
With Louise made the wedding cake.
Pretty, fair, not very tall,
Wrecks your carpets, wall-to-wall.
Lively for adventure, game,
Sets fire to rugs with candle flame.
Loving child and loyal friend,
All virtues now, the vices end,
Although she likes a drop of wine,
I'm more than proud to say she's mine!

And now to Jay I hand our Floss,
For those who don't already know
It's what I've always called her. So …
Heed my advice: the woman's boss!
And if I haven't made that clear,
You always answer, 'Yes, my dear!'
You've made your choice, succumbed to charms,
Confucius always makes one think
That man who sinks in woman's arms
Soon has arms in woman's sink.

You've walked the aisle, reached the altar,
Sung a rousing wedding hymn,
So just remember when you falter,
A woman's pledge 'I'll' 'Alter' 'Him'.
Ah romance! Emotional, one hears,
Even the wedding cake's in tiers!

Enough of this merry digression,
Let us recall the bride's procession,
Caught in time to later treasure
In photos John takes for our pleasure.
Bridesmaids fair in blue and cream,
Floral splendour, rainbow dream.
Tinted ribbons and bouquets,
Nosegays sweet from Janice Mayes.
Tartan canines, eager, ready,
Jovial Jester, trusty Teddy.

Then our handsome kilted groom,
Kindly, thoughtful, caring, strong,
The bride herself, resplendent bloom,
Devoted, pretty as a song.

We watch them in the bridal march
To Malcolm's rustic wedding arch,

Where the groom and tender spouse
Before us make their nuptial vows.
As witnesses we share this time,
The bonds of wedlock so sublime.

Our gift is love, no greater wealth,
We wish them happiness and good health.
Through life's fierce storms and sunny weather
God grant them many years together.
So let us toast, this festive day,
Our loving couple, Em and Jay!

REMEMBRANCE

Nigh on a Century Born – a Life in Verse

A eulogy narrated at the funeral of my mother.

Florence Stephanie Agnes Player
1914 – 2010

Nigh on a century born,
Little, but of good cheer,
Florence, as Agnes known,
Hester, twin sister dear,

In Westminster, where parliament's found,
With Palace and Abbey resplendent,
And English Kings and Queens are crowned,
'Midst banners, flags and pennant,

Where in starkly contrasting surround
Lived the Webbs in brick, block tenement.
With sisters many and brother one,
She laughed and played and grew,
With Hetty, constant companion,
Was schooled, then taught to sew.

Working in the department store,
When, 'neath the sinister threat of war,
Approaching the age of twenty-four,
She entered St Matthew's hallowed door.
And sparkling white in bridal veil,
Married Idris from Rhondda's dale,
The register entry in writing grand,
"Rank or profession – Dressing Gown Hand".

Then just as the world goes wild,
Agnes is carrying child.
Europe is ablaze,
September, thirty-nine,
Reservists summoned to sign,
Idris rejoins the line.
Prestatyn training days.
Married quarters for fortunate wives
Where Allan, the first-born, soon arrives,
A new life, as others lose their lives.
Idris departs to foreign shore,
Agnes with son to London once more,
Back to her father and mother's door.
The blitz, the bombing, ruin and void,
All to the shelter, home destroyed,
Then moving on to safer domain,
Uncertain path, evacuation:
New Malden, Clevedon, West Bromwich - Gun Lane,
First school for Allan's education.

All things come to an end.
War is no exception.
So much to heal and mend
As foe becometh friend
And hope will fear transcend,
Tranquillity's conception.
With peace no need for further flight.
Agnes returns to find, once more,
Her London life, to reunite
With Idris, soldier back from war,
To fill the six-year darkest night
With peacetime's iridescent light.

A soldier's pay put aside,
A house in New Malden bought,
Though likely to subside
From a rocket bomb onslaught.
Repairs are made to home, and life,
So much damage from the strife,
Now Agnes, once again the wife,
Is now, once more, the loving mother
As Allan gains a little brother,
And Idris tries to make his mark
As tradesman grocer in Raynes Park.
With both boys now at school,
And Agnes behind the counter,
Idris turns to milking stool!
Off to run a dairy cool
In Swindon sells his pinta!
In just two years the business fails.
Agnes supports her man from Wales,
Staying here and there, until
The Players move to Burgess Hill.

Chanctonbury Road,
Our own three bedroomed semi,
A permanent abode
(As permanent as any).
The year is nineteen fifty-four,
The family finally settles down.
In hospital and factory floor
Mum works, as dad commutes to town.
John is at school, a happy learner,
Allan starts work as fitter and turner.
Agnes cares for us all,
The family's strength and heart.
Idris hears welfare's call,
In social work a start.

Allan enters his life's career,
Heating, ventilating engineer.
The years roll by, the boys depart,
Allan to build a house and wed,
John to study the teacher's art,
Agnes and Idris again move bed
To Caterham, but not too keen,
So back to Sussex, Goddard's Green,
And then a summons from the Queen!
For pension work, Dad's charity,
Investiture – the M.B.E.
Off to the Palace all four travel,
(And an O.B.E. for Jimmy Savile!?!?)
But how to address them properly,
Now they're the family's flagship?
Why, your Uncle Idris M.B.E.
And, of course, your Auntie Ag-ship.
(An attribution, you'll recall
We owe to Geoff and Johnny Hall.)

The green retirement years,
Garden, home and friends,

Then mother's noble tears
As Idris' lifespan ends.
So once again back to the city
To Watney's Mortlake flat with Hetty.
The widows two, peas in a pod,

On ballroom dance floor, steps they trod,
Ever busy, hale and hearty,
Off to eightieth birthday party.
In touch with children, sisters all,
And both great grannies, very small,
But woe to the tradesman, for his sins,
Who thought to cross the fierce Webb twins.

The century draws to a close,
The twins in their eighty-sixth year,
The river of time ever flows,
Ere long she has lost Hetty dear.
Allan and Zelma take her home,
As mind and thoughts begin to roam,
To Suffolk then, her final days,
In kindly care home, 'neath sun's rays.
Then life's soft spirit's peaceful ebb,
For Florence Stephanie Agnes Webb.

But now she lives on in us all,
As memory comes to the fore,
For each of us can recall,
The Agnes that we adore.
And as she looks down from on high
Some facts in which to delve,
Nine grandchildren say goodbye,
And great-grandchildren twelve.
There were sisters eight and brother one,
Innumerable nephews and nieces
Children just two, Allan and John,
But both have done well for the species.
In-law daughters started with Jenny,
She held them in fondness tender,
But thought there were rather too many,
So we stopped at Zelma and Brenda.

Though lacking education,
Not knowing verb or tense,
She rose above her station
With a degree in common sense.
Her wit was sharp, her judgement sound,
She kept both feet upon the ground,
When dad was talking she knew her place,
But spoke in volumes with her face.

She wouldn't suffer fools,
We called her the Old Growler.
She broke grammatical rules
With a frequent verbal howler.
Producing an unending crop
Of words from Mrs Malaprop.
Thus, the sick went into extensive care,
With Casanova of the liver,
And cold sore salad she'd prepare,

For the delicate essence to deliver.
But that is why we loved her,
And where this tribute ends.
We thank you all for being here,
Our family and friends.
Oh, by the way, she hated spuds,
Much preferring marrow,
So, the final epithet is dad's,
"Our plucky little sparrow."

JOHN PLAYER

<u>Tony Lewis</u>

On the unexpected death in April 2023 of my good friend, Tony, who I met soon after I arrived in Suffolk in 1982.   We shared many fine times together.

We miss you, beautiful man from Wales,
Your wit, your joyfulness, your smile.
Together we told a thousand tales
From forty years, as we go back a while.

So much we shared, our leftist leaning,
The village cricket club reformed,
At the Stonham Dog so oft convening
Where gifted children all performed.

For youngsters, too, a chess club thriving,
Matches played around the land.
Where's Perkins had the villagers jiving,
Two Johns, two Tonys had formed a band.

In the land of our fathers your late years were spent,
Our visits were rare, as distance entails.
But with Leo, at last, you were fully content,
Never happier Tony, our dear friend from Wales.

RETIREMENT AND FAREWELL

Elaine

A sonnet written for Elaine Smith, colleague, friend and Occupational Health Adviser, on her retirement from Gipping Occupational Health, March 2023

Spring resurgent, flowers yellow, meadows verdant,
Awa' she flies, bonnie Caledonian friend.
She ever was a good and faithful servant.
Always the needs of others, ready to attend.
Elaine and I would plan appointed assignations,
Early morning pick-ups there in Washbrook's street,
Sharing juicy secrets as we drove to destinations,
Secrets that we shared along with everyone we'd meet.
Elaine, we wish you well, so many years have passed
Since we met. And I, as Gipping lorry-ate,
A voice for those present and those of distant past,
We hail thee, Scottish queen, Helena Floreat.
Though now departing, in our hearts you'll e'er remain,
Flower from the Highlands, our treasure, our Elaine.

Alex Ross

On the occasion of Alex's retirement as Head of Department (HoD), Craft,
Design and Technology (C.D.T.) from Stowmarket High School, 1990 – ish.
Alex was a very cheeky chappie, witty, good humoured, and a master of the
double entendre. He would always preface any criticism of the school's senior
management team with the words -
"With the greatest respect, …"

With the greatest respect in the world
We shall soon say farewell to the chap
Who could turn wood, both knotted and knurled,
Into very fine pieces of **cr ...** eative furniture.

On a happy or sorrowful note
Does he leave us, this C.D.T. HoD?
His reply to this question I quote:
"You know I'm a miserable **so** ... and so because I'm retiring."

In his years spent at Stowmarket High,
All the changes he fondly recalls.
Adviser's suggestions he'd try,
Stating this is a load of .. work for my department, but very
worthwhile.

The children he taught all adored him.
He was loved by each one in the class.
Even ruffians and rogues would applaud him,
And he thought them a **pain** ... fully sad group of youngsters.

He looked after equipment with care,
Putting all tools away, he would lock up.
If you broke a machine he'd forbear
From describing your fault as a **c** ... hronic error of judgement on
your part.

41

JOHN PLAYER

Famed for verse and poetic devices
Which were read both by wise men and fools,
He wrote innocent words such as vices,
Nuts, knockers, screws, cobblers and tools.

When new female staff were appointed,
Alex showed all his charm and his wits.
He was helpful and kind while he pointed
Attention to the shape of their **t** ... eaching career prospects.

His requests were all made 'with permission'.
He refused to mock, jeer, boo or hiss.
Respecting those in high position,
He was never heard taking the ... Headmaster to task.

He spent early years on Safari.
Painting wildlife he'd patiently sit.
"Uchafu" he'd call out in Swahili,
Which, loosely translated means **s** ... illy me! I've spilt paint all over
the canvas.

His departure we all view with sorrow.
He really will sadly be missed.
He won't be in school on the morrow,
So we're all out tonight to get **p** ... resentations and speeches made in
his honour.

And so, Alex Ross we salute you,
The banners and flags are unfurled,
With the kindness and fondness that suit you
And the greatest respect in the world ...

You old bastard!!

Alex's Poetic Response

I've packed my bags, it's time to go,
I feel a little sad, you know.
Old soldiers simply fade away,
But teachers? – Well, what can I say?
With chalk dust trapped in eyes and nose,
And ink and blotting twixt the toes,
Their cane now bent, no longer straight,
You'd think they'd bow to pressing fate.

But never fear, they're sterner stuff,
They'll never say they've had enough.
They'll stand with bent cane at the ready,
Their eyes still bright, their posture steady.
It seems no parting shall befall,
I'll say goodnight – God bless you all.

Alex Ross

An Alphabetical Tribute - 'JJ'

Working in Cambridge on Friday 13th October 2023 with Gipping
Occupational Health Advisor, Janine Jones. This was to be her last few days
with the company.

AA, a sad acronym for Alcoholics Anonymous,
B.B. King, who played the blues and quickly rose to fame.
CC stands for carbon copy, both pieces thus synonymous.
A Doctor of Divinity adds D.D. to his name.
EE, a mobile network, 'Everything Everywhere',
With a love text to your bestie, FF, Forever Friends.
MT GG means Hungry Horse, HH! No hay to spare,
Ii, a place in Finland where the Iijoki river wends. *(honestly!)*
But JJ means one thing alone, the lovely Janine Jones,
Oh, the alphabetical theme stops here, it was rapidly getting worse!
I'll think of her beyond the grave, when I'm just a heap of bones,
A neat and tidy, dedicated, kind and caring nurse.
She leaves this day, she's moving on, a bitter pill to swallow,
Who'll take her place I know not, but she'll be a hard act to follow.

BIRTHDAYS

Iain Armstrong, 40

My friend Iain was Technical Services Manager at TNT Logistics. The song was sung to him by colleagues on the occasion of his 40th birthday to the tune of 'I am the very model of a modern Major General' from the Gilbert and Sullivan opera, 'The Pirates of Penzance'. He shattered his arm in a skiing accident.

Glossary of Technical References

LAN – Local Area Network
VAN – Virtual Area Network
WAN – Wide Area Network

I am the very model of a 'techie' service manager,
I'm lower than director but I'm senior to a janitor,
I've packed my forty years with a hyper of activity,
And never yet allowed myself a period of passivity.
I've specified a traffic system full of facts statistical,
I've managed global networks and an interface logistical,
I've analysed enquiries technical and operational,
And run a Helpdesk managed by a database relational.
(chorus) He's run a Helpdesk managed by a database relational,
He's run a Helpdesk managed by a database relational,
He's run a Helpdesk managed by a data database relational.

I ran the Sandy depot and the I.T. systems Mendlesham,
And now the network infrastructure TNT at Atherstone.
In short in matters VANager and WANager and LANager
I am the very model of a 'techie' service manager.

JOHN PLAYER

In short in matters VANager and WANager and LANager
He is the very model of a 'techie' service manager.

I run around incessantly like sisters in a nunnery,
I love to go to Highbury and watch the players 'Gunnery',
My energy in 5-a-side's a bubble quite unpoppable
And when I run towards the goal, I'm totally unstoppable.
I dearly love the Alpine slopes for reasons unaccountable,
I've yet to find a snowy mountain peak that's insurmountable,
I ski across the hardest runs a figure unmistakeable,
I only wish my Armstrong arms were utterly unbreakable!

His only wish his Armstrong arms were utterly unbreakable,
His only wish his Armstrong arms were utterly unbreakable,
His only wish his Armstrong arms were utter utterly unbreakable.

No matter what, my metal arm has made me more bionical,
Nothing at all can stop me now, despite my fortieth chronicle,
And still in matters VANager and WANager and LANager
I remain the very model of a 'techie' service manager.

And still in matters VANager and WANager and LANager
He is the very model of a 'techie' service manager!

46

Hilary Dearing, 50

My friend Hilary was a colleague at Stowmarket High School who taught Food Technology. On the occasion of her 50th Birthday, I entered the staffroom in a Tarzan outfit, read her this celebratory poem, then whisked her off over my shoulder.

Out of the jungle's steaming vines,
I come with coarse poetic lines,
Full of rapture and elation
To share with you a celebration.
To each there comes a moment when
They'll ne'er see forty-nine again:
The hair grows grey, the stomach sags,
The eyes develop bulbous bags,
The reflexes were once much quicker,
And now the girth's becoming thicker.
The back and shoulders slowly stoop,
And other bits begin to droop.
Sadly, for Tarzan and for Jane
They'll ne'er see forty-nine again.

But what's this I see down in the clearing -
A trim and youthful thing called Dearing,
Far too nimble, quick and nifty
To make you think that she was fifty.
I'll leave old Jane back in the trees
And sweep our Hilly off her knees....

... but I may need some help!

With love from Tarzan.

Zelma Player, 50

On the occasion of my dear sister-in-law Zelma's 50th birthday party in November 2002, my band 'Where's Perkins' played this song to the tune of 'Blackberry Way', originally recorded by 'The Move' in 1970. Zelma had worked as a Health Visitor.

<u>Fifty Today</u>

Fifty today, still visiting the babies in their cots,
The tiny tots.
Still full of life, despite the fact she's Allan Player's wife,
His trouble and strife!
Still making everybody happy
With her Caribbean smile,
So, try aromatherapy now …ow …ow!

Zelma's fifty today,
She's still cooking, cuddly looking.
Zelma's fifty today, having fun when Chelsea play away!

Fifty today, as fine a figure as she left St Kitts,
No wobbly bits!
A firm Zelma rub – will soothe away your every ache and pain,
Oooh, do it again!
It's no use trying to get her angry,
She'll soon put you down with her smile!
So, try aromatherapy now …ow …ow!

Zelma's fifty today,
She's still cooking, cuddly looking.
Zelma's fifty today, having fun when Chelsea play away!

Jim Prior, 70

The late Jim Prior was a family friend and a member of our little group of walkers. He enjoyed good company, food and wine.
'Seven Forty-Five' was a local gourmet restaurant.

Jim's birthday meal we celebrate in 'Seven Forty-Five';
His healthy lifestyle we admire, amazed he's still alive!
He exercises sitting down in case he should perspire,
Then cools off with a Beaujolais, the naughty Mister Prior.

He served the crown in Singapore before we all were born,
And tells us tales of derring-do, the uniforms he's worn.
His batman summoned in the fray amidst the rebel fire,
"For God's sake, fetch my Beaujolais", intrepid Major Prior!

Refrigeration followed as he managed Hubbard's fleet,
Travelling down the motorway his customers to greet.
A hotel meal, a contract signed as business will require,
Then seal the deal with Beaujolais, the canny Mr Prior.

In later years he roamed the aisles in Tesco's superstore,
Helping all the little ladies who find shopping such a chore.
"Where might I find the marmalade?" a poor soul would enquire,
"I think it's near the Beaujolais" said helpful Mr Prior.

He arrives to eat a healthy meal with us his walking friends.
He'll choose the treacle pudding that the waiter recommends,
Then add the custard, cream and ice cream as is his desire,
And top it off with Beaujolais, the gourmet Mister Prior.

He likes to meet his grumpy pals in Stowupland's Retreat,
He cuts down on the alcohol by rising from his seat,
Then off outside to have a fag – he'll set himself on fire,
Then put it out with Beaujolais, the genial Mister Prior.

JOHN PLAYER

And yet he's reached the milestone of three score years and ten!
He is the perfect, loving dad for Libby, Tom and Ben,
With Annie in Mudd Hall he rose to be the village squire,
So, let's raise a glass of Beaujolais to our hearty friend Jim Prior!

Tammy's Birthday

*Tammy Davies, Finance Officer at Gipping Occupational Health
and resident of Mendlesham. Tammy was somewhat over thirty when I wrote
this grovelling apology.*

October 2023

I missed poor Tammy's birthday.
I'm feeling such a heel.
I'll have to grovel, bow and scrape,
Drop to the floor and kneel.
She's such a lovely lady,
She pays me loads of cash.
So, when she reaches thirty!!!
I'll throw a birthday bash.

My phone is low on battery,
I'll close before it dies.
With luck she'll fall for flattery
Despite the porky pies.
I hope her dogs don't bite me,
Attack me in a rage,
And show consideration
For someone of my age.

I never thought I'd say this,
My payslip always triggers
Sweet thoughts of Tammy Davies,
She's just so good at figures.

HIGH DAYS AND HOLIDAYS

To celebrate Brenda's 70th birthday we took a river cruise down the Danube. I wrote this sonnet at Budapest's Ferenc Liszt Airport while our flight home was delayed. I reflected on the journey through the airport as well as the cruise itself.

Majesty of the Danube

The sun scorched the runways of the Airport Franz Liszt,
    As we snaked towards check-in at Terminal Two.
    Sad lovers departing, they tenderly kissed,
    Her prayer that Security would not let **him** through.
    With formalities over, the hard sell commences,
    Cosmetically speaking; Versace, Chanel,
    L'Oréal and Dior all invading our senses
    With ludicrous pricing, and all for a smell!
As we board our flight homeward, we think of the River
    Which brought us to cities of silver and gold,
Of Kings, Queens and Emperors whose deeds make us quiver,
    And tales of invasions which turned the blood cold.
Yet the poor ones who suffered, their children now greet us,
    And with proud generosity, they welcome and treat us.

A ROYAL CELEBRATION

A sonnet written on the occasion of the Coronation of King Charles III and Queen Camilla on 6th May 2023. The door to the Chapter House in Westminster Abbey is thought to be the oldest in England, dated by dendrochronologists to the reign of King Edward the Confessor, circa 1050.

The Old Saxon Door

From a mighty Saxon oak tree, a wooden door is made,
Traced back nigh on a thousand years, just as our royal line,
Surviving yet in Abbey with thirty monarchs laid,
Westminster, Royal Peculiar, Edward Confessor's shrine.
The burial place of scholars, poets, the Warrior Unknown,
The scientist, the lawmaker, all worthy of acclamation.
The seedlings of our culture at its best they each have sown,
But now once more our thoughts are turned to Royal Coronation.
With King and Queen anointed, then crowned in due tradition,
The monarchy remains the keystone of our constitution.
But the King is not elected, he accedes to his position,
With dissenting voice which calls for a republican solution,
Yet the oak door to the Chapter House has stood the test of time,
And with the peal of steadfastness, the Abbey bells will chime.

BOWLS

In 2023, I had the honour of leading a team from Mendlesham Bowls Club to victory in Division 3 of the Stowmarket and District Bowls League.

Played 18, Won 18

Undeterred by fading years, aches, maladies, fatigue,
We put our best foot forward astride the bowling green.
A lowly place, Division Three, Stowmarket District League,
We played for fun, but still we won, eighteen from eighteen.
The lead players set the tone, straight woods from George and Harry,
While Rita, Linda D and Ray outplayed the opposition,
Our skilful skippers, Loranne and Malcolm, Martyn C and Barry,
With Doddy, Guy, the Geymans, Phil and David in addition.
Tough opponents came and went, defeated one by one.
The green? A showpiece, grateful thanks to Simon and his team.
My humble claim as captain? – to get their names all wrong!
Rita's now Loranne and vice versa it would seem!
The season ends; we top the league, a record-breaking run,
League presentation, trophy, but most of all - just fun!

Division 3 Table	Played	Won	Drawn	Lost	For	Against	Points
Mendlesham	18	18	0	0	763	441	112
Borough of Eye	18	12	1	5	752	469	91.5
Great Barton	18	12	1	5	685	523	83.5
Needham Mkt	18	10	0	8	598	572	74
Stowupland	18	10	0	8	603	593	65
Walsham	18	9	0	9	589	606	65
Thorndon	18	9	0	9	632	582	63
Gipping EE	18	5	0	13	549	690	40
Haughley C	18	4	0	14	483	757	29
St Botolphs	18	0	0	18	391	812	1

Dorset

A sonnet written on a family holiday in Dorset in July 2023, reflecting upon my early years in Blandford Forum between 1972 and 1974

Gently tumbling hillside, with hedge-lined narrow lane,
Hillforts from the Iron Age, River Stour fishing,
Memories from distant times, yet now I'm here again,
A fleeting family holiday, yet so much more I'm wishing:
To live with nightjars churring, to wander o'er the heath,
Street Fayre at Milton Abbas, Jurassic fossil beach.
Gazing down from Gold Hill Shaftesbury, Blackmore Vale beneath,
Stately home at Kingston Lacy, avenue of beech.
As Devon and Cornwall tourists pour through on busy highway,
Dorset folk retire inland amidst the harvest crops,
In straw thatch village cottages, with stray sheep on the byway,
While fields of roe and sika deer find refuge in the copse,
In dreams I walk these rolling hills their patchwork fields far
spreading,
My heart and soul once more revived with every step I'm treading.

A Jolly Jaunt

An away day in Huddersfield with friends to watch Ipswich play Huddersfield Town at the John Smith's Stadium.

September 2023

Our merry band of footie fans are off to see the Tow-un,
(It's spoken thus in Suffolk though I've always wondered why.)
There's Steve and Rob, Dan, Malcolm, John, and not forgetting
Truan.
(It's Welsh for miserable wretch, I cannot tell a lie!)
Our first stop is a hedge in Bretton, (Malcolm near to bursting),
And then the Sun Inn Flockton where we all meet up for dinner,
Good pub-grub food, with beer to match, to satisfy our thirsting,
And the long-awaited entrance grand of ill-famed Daniel Skinner.
Customs must be honoured with traditional slap on head,
We lunch with mirth and memories, then taxi to the ground.
Tension as the home team scores. Are we left for dead?
An equaliser, minutes left, we're top of table bound!
A long day spent with weary limbs and drizzling Yorkshire rain,
But we're a jovial, all aged troupe; can't wait to go again!

Elsie

Elsie, our cat, was born in May 2009. She was a rescue kitten. Every day with her is a high day. She is very lively, very affectionate and very funny.

Where are you at, my little cat? You scarce betray your thinking.
With subtle moves and gestures, you hold sway in this house.
We do as we are bidden, obedience without blinking,
Clearing up a heap of feathers, the remnants of a mouse.

Your daily rule is ordered, dictating all the times
When we should rise each morning, when we should go to bed.
You take no note of the pendulum clock, even when it chimes.
At 6 o'clock your morning call, you trample on my head.

You exercise when we do, mad chasing all your toys,
An early morning breakfast, demanding to be fed,
You choose a spot for a morning doze, which every cat enjoys,
Lying feet up on your back pretending to be dead.

You're ever present with us, ofttimes quite unseen,
If sitting on the toilet, you're there beneath my feet.
You help me put the dustbins out, you watch us when we clean,
And when I feed the goldfish, you're with me on the seat.

JOHN PLAYER

The garden is your playground, as well the field beyond,
Leaping up the tree trunks, walking on the fence,
Hunting birds and rodents, staring at the pond.
For us it's mystifying, to you it makes good sense.

At eventide we sit and rest, the programmes make us doze.
You search round for the warmest lap, your claws forever kneading,
You settle here, you settle there, our Elsie comes and goes.
We notice not when she is there or when she is receding,

At ten each night, you leave my lap, your nose points to the stair,
You shoot up to the landing, with us not far behind.
In bed you nuzzle, lick and butt to let us know you care,
You settle us down, your gentle purring helps us to unwind.

You're not a pet, you're one of us, you're sad when we're away.
The catflap leaves you free to roam, there is no fence or cage.
Yet always at the welcome door, whatever time of day,
To complete our threefold family till the passing of our age.

SILLY VERSE

Bishop Cedric

Of Cedric's bishopric at York
The whole episcopate would talk.
When holy Cedric entered orders,
He left six inches round the borders
Of his gown ecclesiastic.
(The tailor didn't use elastic)
He said that at a future date
He might well start to put on weight.

His Bishop's mitre, we are told,
Though fashioned by the Papal Fold
And posted by the Papal Staff
Was made size seven and a half.
It was a splendid, stately mitre,
But Cedric wore a half size tighter.
It therefore perched down on his nose,
Allowing glimpses of his toes.

Thus, when he came to tour his see,
A no-see tour it happ'd to be.
He entered inns and vaults of wine
Instead of church and holy shrine.
The flock he led, it makes one weep,
Was actually a flock of sheep!

The strong and healthy too were healed,
Until he strolled into a field …
His mitre gold, his robes of red
Enticed a bull to raise its head
And charge at our illustrious fool.
Alas this was no Papal Bull.
Poor Cedric soared high, with a twist,
He'd met a bull Nonconformist,
A scion of the Reformation
Which caused our Bishop's expiration.
Thus, he never put on weight
And stands today at Peter's gate.

Limerick

A parson from Mendlesham Green
Always stammered when meeting the Dean.
"Your G-Grace," he would utter,
"If you c-cure my stutter,
I'll rec-recommend you to the Queen."

Alternatively …

A parson from Mendlesham Green
Enjoyed playing chess with the Dean.
But was in his bad books
For calling Knights Rooks
And declaring the Bishop a Queen.

The Cleaner

Best sung to the tune of 'My Old Man's a Dustman'
by **Lonnie Donegan.**

I am the family cleaner,
I clean the household bogs.
They're always blocked 'cos Edmund tends to
Dump such massive logs.

I free them with my bare hands
And clear the pipes within.
It doesn't smell like L'Oréal,
But it's better for my skin.

MODERN TIMES

Inventions

Is a large monk singing bass in the choir
Better known as a Deep Fat Friar?

Even worse than the deep fat frier?
The infernal, abysmal blow-air hand drier.

There's a food-processor in my house,
A micro-processor, complete with mouse.
The hours I save
With a micro-wave.
To complete the quartet, dare I mention
A new, contemporary invention
Recommended by my good friend Dave ...

... a food-wave.

DJ's

Inane DJs are oft heard to spout
"It's five before nine, so check this out!"
Never mind the tattoos and the gurgling voice,
The esoteric music choice
Much worse than arm waving and dyed green hair,
The earring, nose stud and zany wear,
Linguistic imports are hard to bear!
"Listen to this, it's five to nine."
Will do just fine.

Rapping Man

So you wanna make a million then take my advice
And soon you'll be raking in a hefty slice.
You don't need no talent just verbal diarrhoea,
And let the double negatives flow out of your rear.
You don't need no brain and no inter-lect,
You just gotta treat me with respect,
Cos you can talk good and you can really rap,
Though everything you're' sayin' is a load of c**p.

You think you're twenty-four carat but you're talking like a parrot,
You're a'hootin' and a'tootin' and squawking like an owl,
When you're rappin' and a'tappin', point ya' feet like a carrot,
So give it up, rapping man, and throw in the towel!

Just find an old chart topper number one hit
And then while it's playing spout a load of s**t
Just **EMphaSIZE** every **MAJ**or **BEAT**
And all the little kiddies will be tapping their feet.
So, chant in a monotone, composing on the wing,
Your drivel will get nowhere if you try to sing.
You're no opera diva and you know you can't croon,
And the last thing you want is a melodious tune.

You're now just eighteen carat 'cos you're talking like a parrot,
You're a'hootin' and a'tootin' and squawking like an owl,
You're rappin' and a'tappin' point ya' feet like a carrot,
Just give it up, rapping man, and throw in the towel!

You can talk about life with a capital L,
You can talk about garbage and its pungent smell,
You can talk about love and pronounce it lerve,
You can talk total b*****ks if you've got the nerve,

JOHN PLAYER

You can rabbit on for hours about nothing at all,
And you don't need no tune just a mindless drawl.
Just pronounce words like constipashuurrrn
And very soon you'll be a big sensashurrrn.

**Now you're just nine carat, you keep talking like a parrot,
You're a'hootin' and a'tootin' and squawking like an owl,
You're rappin' and a'tappin' point ya' feet like a carrot,
Won't you give it up, rapping man, and throw in the towel!**

Twenty-four, then eighteen, and now you're just nine.
You'll soon be zero Rapping Man, you're fast in decline!
Will your next chart topper get to number one?
No, the times they are a'changin', and you'll soon be done!

**Now you're zero carat, you're still talking like a parrot,
With your hootin' and a'tootin' and squawking like an owl,
Your rappin' and a'tappin' pointed feet like a carrot,
Dammit, give it up, rapping man and chuck in the towel!**

Flat-Pack Assembly

Fine furniture, though not too dear,
Is sold in flat-packs by IKEA.
They've stores from Aberdeen to Wembley
And specialise in home assembly.
To save us getting in a tether,
Putting cabinets together,
Fitting this small piece to that,
Why not sell goods already flat?
Specialise in doors and kippers,
After Eights and carpet slippers,
Dinner trays and crêpe suzettes,
Wafers thin and fishing nets,
Birthday card and tablemat,
All essentially flat.
So that's that!

But every time I do a job,
I mess it up, or screw it,
Then I remember Mister Punch –
That's the way to do it!

Then as I wash my hands, I hope
To recommend a brand of soap.
With other soap bars worn to vapour,
Imperial Leather leaves a piece of paper.

<u>CAUTIONARY TALES</u>

Two poems written for morning assemblies at Stowmarket High School.

Reginald Pye

Herein the tale of Reginald Pye,
A former pupil at Stowmarket High,
In most regards, a student model,
Learning facts, he found a doddle,
Always top of every class,
GCSE's? - an A+ pass
In fourteen subjects. Reg was not,
However, what you'd call a swot.
He didn't need to sweat or toil,
Or burn away the midnight oil.
If chums called round on any day,
Reg ditched his homework books to play
Some music by his favourite band.
He always found some time on hand,
Which he employed to useful ends,
Winning over many friends
Who sang his praises, hale and hearty,
The life and soul of every party.
Reg was clever, Reg was cool,
The best liked boy in all the school,
Witty, charming, ever a laugh,
Student hero, applauded by staff.
Always earning glowing reports
And Reg was even good at sports!
Soccer player, first fifteen
At rugger, captain – hockey team.

GIPPING JOURNEYS

Whether holding bat or ball
At cricket, he was best of all.
Handsome even, six foot tall,
For Reggie all the girls would fall.
Cross your heart and hope to die
Just for a date with Reginald Pye!

His all-round prowess made one wince
To such extent that Mrs Ince,
Who helped the students with their careers,
Predicted many successful years
Ahead for Reg. A level GCE,
And then a first-class Honours Degree
Soon followed by a Ph.D.
At Cambridge University,
Just like Dr. Montgomery,
Then headteacher of Stowmarket High
Throughout the years of Reginald Pye.
Thus, from Suffolk's scholarly cloister
Reg would emerge – the world his oyster.

There was, however, a minor flaw
In Reggie's make-up, nothing more,
A character fault, a tiny blot
In one who otherwise had the lot.
Yet therein we can quickly plot
Our subject's downfall from on high,
Where just as in a moonlit sky
He shone, Stowmarket's brightest star.
The further the drop, the higher you are.
Although a vice scarce worth a mention,
I draw it now to your attention,
Because it ruined Reggie's life,
Losing his friends, his job, his wife.

It left him feeling sad and bitter,
And all because he would drop litter.

Reg began this downward trend
When he borrowed a pencil from a friend,
After having chewed the end,
He dropped it on the classroom floor.
Both friend and pencil were no more.
Not long after, the laughing bunch
Of Year 10 pupils eating lunch,
(Sandwiches in the canteen)
With Reggie were no longer seen.
Deserting Reg, now left alone
In a scrappy heap of chicken bone,
Bread crusts, crisps and apple core
Scattered around him on the floor.
Word went round, "Don't sit with Pye,
It's like pigs eating in a sty."

The time arrived for year-end mock
Examinations, so a lock
Was fitted to the Common Room door.
"You're now to use Room 24!"
And so they did, including Reg,
But very soon, on window ledge,
On desk lids, shelves all round the class
Were paper wrappers, mud and grass,
Chewing gum and bits of cake
Following in Reggie's wake.
Mr Taylor and his form
Considered this above the norm
For rubbish on their classroom floor,
He threw them out and locked the door.
Fellow students asked, "Who is to blame?"
When someone shouted out a name:

"Reginald Pye", no more, no less,
"Wherever he goes, he leaves a mess."
And so Reg fell into disfavour
Through thoughtlessness, not misbehaviour.

Plagued with the litterbug's disease,
It seemed as if the lad had flees.
Recognising this infestation,
Reg was kept in isolation.
Playground chums for many a year,
Spotting Reg would steer well clear.
His girlfriend left him, "Litterlout",
She cried, "if you think I'm going out
With you, you're very much mistaken.
You're just a pig and I don't eat bacon."

On the soccer field some weeks before,
The first eleven had failed to score,
When a shot fired at the opponent's goal
Deflected off a sausage roll
And Cola can, Reggie's morning snack
Which he'd dropped on the pitch. His own right back
And captain called "Bring on the sub.
He's going off, and so's his grub!"
At which he threw the empty tin
At Reggie's head and bruised his chin.
Despite his skill and soccer brain,
Reg never played for the school again.

His later years were very sad,
A tragedy for a talented lad.
A life so full of promise and hope,
He swiftly slid down the slippery slope
To rack and ruin. The blame was placed
On a chronic failure to dispose of waste

JOHN PLAYER

In a litter bin. When out at work
He lost job after job through this sorry quirk.
Starting Monday, sacked by Friday,
He just couldn't keep an office tidy.

His marriage had seemed a perfect match.
His lovely wife was quite a catch.
Smart, attractive, much admired,
Yet even she at last grew tired
Of chasing Reg with brush and mop,
Clearing litter he used to drop.
Feeling unable to stay the course,
She went to court to seek divorce,
Using grounds for her petition
Reggie's squalid disposition.
As decreed by English law
Reg stood up in the dock and swore
To tell the truth. By oath now bound,
He tossed the Bible on the ground.
The judge called out, "I've seen enough.
This man is an untidy scruff."
"But I object!" young Reggie chanted.
"Overruled! – Petition granted."

Shortly after the separation,
Reg discovered his true vocation.
He became the man who works the pump
At the corporation rubbish dump.
Rotting vegetables and paper
Giving off an odorous vapour.
Reggie syphoned from a tank
Into a sewer foul and dank.
After a day the little fool
Transgressed the strict no smoking rule.
He tossed the match into the drain ...

... Poor Reg was never seen again.

This tale has a short P.S.
To those who live a life of mess:
Cast aside this wretched sin,
And ALWAYS use a wastepaper bin!

Trevor Bunn

I tell a tale of a learned fool,
A former student at this school,
Who, while endowed with an Einstein brain,
Allowed a tragic fault to reign,
To wit, his homework was left undone.
Therein the downfall of Trevor Bunn.
As gifted as an Oxford don,
In every respect he far outshone
His fellow pupils. Sharp and bright,
The leading literary light
Of all the Sixth Form was our Trevor.
A child so inestimably clever
That, even with the utmost endeavour,
The other students just couldn't compete
With this scion of the academic elite.

Trevor was clothed with gifts from God.
With intellectual shoes was shod,
Laced with brains, not one could fill'em,
Not Sharon Waspe, nor Lucy Gillam
Nor Miss Burgoyne or Master Pierce.
For though the competition was fierce,
Trevor's glowing erudition
Quickly dispelled the opposition.
Despite his A Grades, Jason Barrow
Was, next to Trevor, a vegetable marrow.
While Nigel Wilson, a member of Mensa,
Was deemed considerably denser.

So, in a word young Trevor was smart,
But sadly hadn't acquired the art
Of uninterrupted concentration.
His studies were plagued by deviation.

A sound or movement, voice or action
Would cause immediate distraction.
Thus, if while studying Newton's Law
A spider passed across the floor
By Trevor's desk, he'd stop and gaze.
His work would enter a dormant phase.
In the parlance of the racing horse,
He needed blinkers to stay the course.

But even worse, as he studied alone,
To the lure of friends our Trevor was prone.
He would start to write but very soon
A voice would cry "Let's play pontoon!"
"Behind me Satan", he should have said,
But stones are quickly turned to bread.
Trevor would yield to such temptation,
Leaving his work for another occasion.
But he who succumbs reaps doom and gloom
From the fleshpots of the Common Room.

And so our hero failed to do
The coursework set by teachers who,
Just as the Staffing Handbook states,
Directed their fire at Mr. Yates,
The Sixth Form Tutor. He heard their moans
And railed at Trevor in Yorkist tones.
"Now listen and take notice, Bunn,
Homework's set and must be done.
If you fail to produce another assignment
I'll place you in solitary confinement.
Even worse, with the power I wield,
I'll fix you a job in 'Uddersfield."
But even threats as dire as these
Blew past Trevor like a breeze.
In class the picture was just as bad

He drove his subject teachers mad,
Demonstrating his petty vice
In history lessons with Miss Le Grys
For once, as she explained the cause
Of one of those tedious civil wars
That have besmirched the distant past,
Trevor's eye was keenly cast
Down to the playground far below
Where people wandered to and fro,
Some of them fast, and others slow.
Just then the dustcart motored by
Catching Trevor's roving eye
As Miss Le Grys revealed the facts
Concerning Charles' shipping tax.
"What do you think of the King and why?"
She asked. "It's rubbish", came Trevor's reply.

In time his mental aberration
Suffered further deterioration.
As well as allowing his mind to stray
From the subject at hand, there came a day
When his pen followed suit. He started to doodle,
Covering his notes with spaghetti and noodle,
Squares and circles, hearts and hoops,
Loping lines and linear loops.
To wit his new mathematics book
Assumed a strange aesthetic look,
Mixing the matrix and simple equation
With avant-garde delineation.
While decimal and vulgar fraction
Grew out of Dali-esque abstraction.
All of which entangled mess
Caused Mr. Dawson much distress.
"Now listen Bunn," he tersely cried,
"The subject maths, pure and applied,

Is not for those of artistic bent.
Take this twaddle to Mr. Kent."

It further troubles me to mention
That Trevor's failure to pay attention
Nearly ruined the Sixth Form Production.
As Mrs. Payne was giving instruction
And busy rehearsals were under way,
Trevor was given a part to play.
As well as speaking a line or two,
He also had to appear on cue,
Which he continually failed to do.
Whenever wanted he couldn't be found.
People searched but he'd gone to ground,
Or made some meaningless excursion
Occasioned by a minor diversion.
Mrs. Payne would shout, "Does anyone
Know the whereabouts of that fool Bunn?"
But no-one did save Trevor alone,
For he'd wandered off in a world of his own
And, like as not, he'd then be seen
Staring at the washing machine
In the H.E. room as it whirled around.
On another occasion he was found
At 3pm in the Dinner Queue
A singularly pointless thing to do.
He lost his part and, in a rage,
Mrs. P. told Trevor to sweep the stage,
To clear the boards of dust and mess,
A task he performed with some success,
Much to everybody's delight,
Until it came to opening night.
The hall was full, the stage was set,
The nervous cast began to fret.
The house lights dimmed, the music played,

Act one, scene one, enter the maid,
Stage left, in the drawing room,
When in sweeps Trevor, with his broom.

The days passed by, but all too soon
There came the fateful month of June,
When GCE examinations
Cause nervousness and palpitations.
Now many staff had voiced their fears
Over Trevor's record, the last two years.
Despite attempts to throw him out
He was given the benefit of the doubt.
Since natural talent was on parade,
Five 'A' level entries had been made
On Trevor's behalf, based on the hope
That with his brains the lad could cope.
The testing moment had begun.
Forename Trevor, surname Bunn,
Candidate number 0-2-1,
Subject, paper number, date,
He set off at a cracking rate,
But as he paused to contemplate
The rubric for the opening section,
His mind flew off in a new direction,
Transcendental meditation
Took the place of concentration.
Drifting leisurely into space
He imagined himself in another place.
He thought of home, he thought of friends,
He thought of a million odds and ends,
He thought of several anagrams,
But he didn't think about exams.
He read the writing on his table,
He doodled on the number label,
He gazed at every passer-by,

Observing the progress of a fly
As it flew upon the windowpane
And then flew back to his desk again,
Upon his pencil case alighting
When a teacher said, "Will you please stop writing".
Three hours had vanished into vapour,
And Trevor had written his name on the paper.
His other exams were much the same.
He did some doodles and wrote his name,
That is, of course, when he actually came.
On four occasions he failed to arrive
Seduced by some alternative.
Like cockroach racing, watching a drip,
Or prising open a paper clip.
Lured by syrens such as these,
No bonds could hold our Ulysses.

With his academic career in shreds
He sought a living selling beds,
And found a lucrative position,
With basic pay and good commission,
Working on the second floor
At a well-known, local furniture store.
Now from the window he could see
The pleasant, rustic scenery.
He paused a while to count some sheep,
Lay on a bunk and fell asleep.
The foreman said, "My, you look tired,
Well wake up son, you've just been fired".
But let me not bore you to tears,
With Trevor's other failed careers.
For now, at last he's reached his goal,
Lifelong diversion on the dole
Devoid of pressure, stress, or fears
No doubt he'll live for ninety years.

GIPPINGS JOURNEYS

Printed in Great Britain
by Amazon

45040896R00055